Special thanks to:

Samuel Daniels,
Mikeala Patterson and Woodridge State High School.

ISBN 978-0-6451525-8-6

First Printed in 2021
©Copyright 1000 Tales

All rights reserved.
This book or any portion thereof may not be reproduced, stored in or introduced in a retrieval system, or transmitted, in any form or by any means without the express written permission of 1000 Tales Co-op Ltd except for the use of brief quotations in a book review.

Photography by
Ameera Karimshah
Atiya Karimshah
Sam Daniels
Mikeala Patterson
Nathan Lyons
Daniel Goli
Hanan Dajan
John Udzodinma
Julie Fischart
Katrina Patindol
Maria Iskander
Samanthra Govender

General enquiries
Info@1000tales.org.au

Shop
www.1000tales.org.au

About This Book

Everyone has a story to tell.

This has always been our philosophy but breaking down the social and cultural barriers to get people to open up is hard. So we find things everyone can relate to and then we stand back and we listen.

Food is one of those things. It has a way of bringing people together, of evoking memories and emotions.

It tells a story.

Whether it's the first dish you taught yourself to cook or that age-old recipe passed down through the generations, it's a story of innovation, culture, necessity and so much more. Cooking tells us stories of journeys taken, of generations past, of love and homes with roots that touch every continent in the world.

We can't think of a better way to celebrate the diversity, creativity and tradition found in our beautiful country.

Join us on this journey into the lives and homes of everyday Australians.

We would like to acknowledge the Traditional Custodians of the continent of Australia. Whose cultures are among the oldest living cultures in human history and whose languages and knowledge have infused and inhabited this land for millennia.

We recognise their continuing connection to the land, waters and culture and we pay our respects to their Elders past, present and emerging.

Table of Contents

Curried Sausages	8
Pongal (Sweet Rice)	10
Aloo Gobi	14
Pepper Soup	18
Ponded Yam	19
Macaroni Cheese	22
Libyan Aseeda	25
Pan Fry	26
Chelo Kabob	29
Garkic Soy Chicken	31
Pecel	34
Bobotie	38
Khan Family Kebabs	42
Nasi Goreng	46
Kare Kare	51
Butter Chicken	53
Kakh Biscuits	56
Egyptian Feta Omlette	58
Lamb Curry Bunny Chow	59

Nathan Lyons

I'm Nathan Lyons, 35 from Sydney, I grew up in the inner city suburb of Glebe, raised by a single mother from about the age of 10 with 3 other siblings. I grew up in social housing. Money was tight back then so we were taught from a young age to shop cheap and going to stores such as jewel and buying the home brand items.

My favorite dishes growing up were; Curried sausages, Meatloaf, Anything Chicken.

I make Curried Sausages in my family so my kids now enjoy the same recipe that I was taught by my uncles and aunties. Being a cheap and simple meal to make it is definitely a favorite amongst my kids. It's one of those recipes that can be changed up to suit the fussiest of eaters. A simple way I change it up is changing it from beef sausages to pork, lamb, chicken or kangaroo sausages.

Curried sausages for me brings back so many memories. Sitting with the cousins, listening to Charlie Pride while eating dinner being yelled at by my auntie, to eat all our food. She slaved over the oven all day to make us dinner. Growing up it was definitely a staple meal in my household but also in all my relatives homes as well. I think it's one of those meals many members across our community can identify with and remember having and still have regularly.

This is one of the recipes that has been handed down through the generations and Curry powder is a must for every Indigenous household. So the classic curried sausages for me is one meal that the community, my family and I always have and always will enjoy. I look forward to the day I can make this for my grandchildren and the next generation. It doesn't matter where I am in Australia, when this recipe is made it brings the mob together, and mob means home even if I'm not on my own country/traditional lands.

Curried sausages, a classic Australian family favorite and comfort food, thick rich gravy, delicious vegetables and is preferably served with buttery fluffy mashed potato just the way mum made it.

Curried Sausages

INGREDIENTS

8 Sausages
2 tablespoons Oil
1 small Onion - sliced
1-2 tablespoons Curry powder
2 tablespoons Flour
2 cups Chicken Stock
1 cup Frozen Peas, corn and carrot
2 tablespoons thick Cream

INSTRUCTIONS

Place sausages into a pot of boiling water and simmer for five minutes. Let cool, de-skin and slice into 5cm pieces.
Heat oil in a large frying pan and fry onions for 3 minutes.
Add in the curry powder, fry for a further 2 minutes then mix through the flour. Pour in the stock and return the sausages to the pan.
Bring to the boil, stirring continuously, and simmer for 15-20 mins, Add the peas and cream five minutes before serving

Pongal (Sweet Rice)

The Author of this story did not wish to be identified.

Once a year in Tamil culture, people come together to celebrate 'Thai Pongal', which is a thanksgiving festival focused on thanking the sun for the year's harvest.
During the celebration many traditional dishes are prepared including Pongal; a delicious sweet and milky rice dish.

In 2016, I married my now husband who came to Australia years earlier when seeking asylum from the Sri Lankan Civil War. Since being married, we've had two beautiful children and enjoy spending time together as a family.
As someone who fled his homeland, sweet Pongal is a dish that brings back memories to my husband of his upbringing. He shares stories of Thai Pongal when his family would come together to make the dish and share it amongst themselves, extended family and others in their village. Pongal was cooked by his various different family members, but most often by his father whom he learnt the dish from.
Now as he lives in Australia with myself and our two children, he often cooks Pongal on weekends for our family's breakfast. The dish has become a symbol that connects my husband back to his homeland and culture, and in bringing Pongal to our family home he has also taught me, someone brought up in Australia how to cook it. Cooking Pongal is also something we hope to pass on to our children when they are old enough, in the meantime it's a dish that's very much enjoyed by our toddler!

Recipe

Ingredients (amounts will vary depending on cooking pot size):
Basmati rice (uncooked)
Milk (we use regular cow's milk, but you can also use other types including coconut milk)
Sugar (raw or white)
2-3 pinches of salt
Optional extras: cashew nuts and/or dry fruits (such as currants, raisins, dates or shredded coconut)

Method:
Fill a small cooking pot about one sixth full with uncooked basmati rice.
Pour milk over the rice until the pot is just over halfway full.
add sugar, starting with around 1/8 of a cup. As the mixture starts to cook you can use a clean spoon to taste test and add more sugar depending on your taste preference.
Also add 2-3 pinches of salt.
Cook on a stovetop on low to medium heat, stirring often so the rice doesn't stick or burn to the bottom.
As the milk evaporates you may need to add more to avoid the rice becoming too dry- you want to aim for a creamy consistency coating the rice by the time it has finished cooking.
\If you are wanting to add any cashews and/or dry fruits, add when the rice is around 3 quarters cooked.
the rice is soft, but not overcooked, it will be ready to serve. You may wish to sprinkle each serving with more dry fruits and/or cashew nuts.
Taste and enjoy!

Samuel Daniels

I was born in Brisbane, Australia but was lucky enough to have travelled widely during my childhood. From a young age I was exposed to many different cultures across Asia and the pacific. I have continued my love of travel ever since and have immensely valued exploring different cultures and ways of thinking as I have grown. I believe it has played a pivotal role in shaping who I am today.

My favourite dish growing up, which I still make today, is an Aloo Gobi style curry that my dad used to make. I could only start eating this dish when I was about 14 years old as it was very spicy for me as a child. Once I finally gave it a go though, it instantly became my favourite dish and I slowly learned how to perfect it myself. My mouth waters every time I think of having it for dinner and because the dish was typically made to feed our whole family, I still haven't learnt how to downsize the recipe, which means now that I am older, I am still cooking it for a family of six even though its usually just for me! It means plenty of left overs for the week ahead!

The dish was my dads take on the traditional potato and cauliflower Aloo Gobi curry from India, but my dad would add extra ingredients like almonds, mustard seeds and lots of lemon.

Aloo Gobi

2- 3 Potatoes – chop into bite size chunks and boil until just soft.
1 Cauliflower – chop into small florets
Grate a handful of ginger
Finely chop 4-5 garlic cloves
1-2 Red chillies – finely chop
1-2 Handfuls of natural almonds
1 litre of yoghurt
3-4 Lemons
Small handful of mustard seeds
Garam Masala powder
Turmeric powder
1 Bunch of coriander

Boil the potatoes until they are just soft and set aside.
Over a hot frying pan or wok, add the almonds, ginger, garlic, mustard seeds and chilli.
Cook until soft & roasted (3-4 mins).
Add the cauliflower and continue (3-4 mins).
Add the softened potatoes and sprinkle of a generous amount of garam masala and turmeric powder – stir to combine.
Add the yoghurt and lemon juice and stir to combine – turn the heat on the frying pan or wok to low or off and let settle for 5-10 minutes.
Finish with a generous amount of coriander.
Eat!

John Uzodinma

My name is Uzodinma John, I am from Nigeria which is located at the west part of Africa. With my culture, one fundamental uniqueness about it is that my culture accommodates and respect the dignity of being human. I moved into Australia in 2018 and I am still in the process of learning Australian cultures and its way of living.

My favourite dish growing up as a child is called the Pepper soup and ponded yam. My mum does the cooking most times, and my elder sisters. What makes this dish special is the feeling of taste you get after eating, more so, the good health benefit which makes it the most preferred in occasions. The significant of this food for example in occasion, gives the visitor the feeling of a warm reception or that their visit is well appreciated.

Pepper Soup

The first dish is called Pepper Soup, we make this for big and small occasions. You can make this with either goat meat, fish, or chicken depending on what you want. Also, you can make with different kinds of meat of your choice put together and in this case it is called assorted Pepper soup.

Spices, goat meat, chicken gullet, cow intestine.
Goat meat and chicken gullet spiced with Maggi cube and little salt.
Add Spring onion
Pepper Soup spices made from native ingredients
Stir together and cover to cook for 15mins

Note: Do not include water after stir and cover, the meat cooks with its water. In this way, the spices get into the meat very well.
Check on the meat after the stated time to see the quantity of water from the meat, and to add more water depending on your choice and also the hardness of the meat.
Cook for another 30 to 40 minutes depending on how soft or hard you want your meat to be.
Add basil and chilli for flavour. And cook for another 5 minutes.

Tastes as good as it looks!

Ponded Yam

This is called yam. It can be prepared in different ways but for this process, I will take you through on how to make yam porridge.

Yam cut in cubes, ingredients, red or palm oil made from palm nuts.
Blended spices, red oil, shrimp mix and Maggi stock cube mix with the yam.
Add some water to the level with the yam or a little but above and cook for 30 to 40 minutes.
Turn and allow to cool.

Mikeala Patterson

When I was little I didn't want to eat meat. It wasn't because of taste, or texture or a political choice. I just was born not
wanting to eat meat. I also didn't like Brussel Sprouts. Yuck.

I grew up in New Zealand at the bottom of the South Island. It was bitterly cold during the winter. I remember Mum trying to tell me a seafood dish was macaroni but I knew it wasn't. I think she was trying to trick me.

Dad used to make toffee and coconut ice for treats. Mum would cook a chocolate and vanilla steam pudding which I loved but my absolute favourite dish was homemade macaroni cheese.

I used to make it for my children and still cook it now. There are many things I can't remember but I will always remember homemade macaroni cheese.

Macaroni Cheese

The recipe is my own, made up as I go. Flour, butter, cheese, Milk, breadcrumbs.

Classic Macaroni Cheese

400g macaroni

50g butter

2 tbsp plain flour

2 cups milk

2 cups grated cheese

Boil the macaroni as per the instructions on the packet and then drain them.

In a separate saucepan melt the butter.
Add in the flour and mix until thoroughly combined.
Gradually add in milk until smooth.
Remove from heat and add cheese.
Stir until all the cheese is melted.
Pour mixture over drained macaroni and stir until combined.

Pour mixture into an oven proof baking dish.
Sprinkle grated cheese on top and place under grill until cheese is melted and golden in colour.

Hanan Dajan

My name is Hanan Dajan, and I am originally from Libya. My family first arrived in Australia in 1990 and I was born two years later in 1992. Growing up in Australia, I grew up learning about many different cultures. My parents taught us how to speak Arabic and taught us many things about our Libyan culture. My favourite dish growing up in my family was Aseeda and it continues to be my favourite Libyan dish. It is full of flavour, delicious, and comforting. Aseeda is made differently across the Middle East. Growing up, my mother would cook Aseeda on Eid days and on special occasions. It is a dish that requires a great deal of effort to make. I closely observed how my mother made it and learnt how to make it from her. This dish is so special because in Libya this is the dish that is presented to guests and it is also the dish that is served for every momentous occasion such as the birth of a child, graduations, the recovery of a sick person, and all other momentous occasions. In Libya, Aseeda plays a significant role in bringing people together, raising their spirits and celebrating the beauty of life.

Libyan Aseeda

Ingredients:

4 cups of water
½ a teaspoon of salt
1 tablespoon of olive oil
3 ½ cups of plain white or wholemeal flour
1 cup of boiling water
½ cup of boiling water
Honey or Date Syrup
Butter

Method:

Place 4 cups of water in a large sized saucepan. Pour 1 tablespoon of olive oil and ½ a teaspoon of salt. Bring the water to a boil.

Carefully add 3 ½ cups of flour to the boiling water. Stir the mixture quickly with wide/flat wooden spoon. Stir until the dough becomes thick then quickly remove the pot from the heat.

The dough then needs to be mixed. There are two options for mixing the dough. The dough can be mixed using a dough mixer or can be mixed the traditional Libyan way. The traditional way involves placing the pot on the floor against a wall and holding the pot in place with both feet. Slippers are worn on both feet and a tea towel is used to cover the feet and slippers. The dough is then stirred thoroughly with a wooden spoon until the dough softens and becomes lump free.

If the dough was placed in a dough mixer, then return the dough to the saucepan and add 1 cup of boiling water. If the dough was mixed in the traditional way, simply place the pot back on the stove and add 1 cup of boiling water. Turn the heat on low. Break the dough into small/medium pieces with the wooden spoon while the dough is inside the pot. Continue stirring the dough while it is cooking. Once all the water evaporates, turn the heat off.

Place the dough back into the dough mixer and mix it again until it softens and becomes thick or mix the dough again using the traditional way.

After mixing the dough, return the dough into the saucepan or if mixed the traditional way, place the pot with the dough back on the stove. Add ½ cup of boiling water this time and turn the heat on low. Break up the dough into small/medium pieces in the pot. Continue stirring the dough while it is cooking until all the water evaporates.

After all the water evaporates, place the dough into the dough mixer or mix it the traditional way one last time. Mix the dough until it becomes thick and has the consistency of soft play dough.

Allow the dough to cool for 5-10 minutes then shape the dough into a small mound in a large bowl. Create a small circular hole in the middle of the Aseeda with a spoon.

Pour desired amount of melted butter as a shallow moat around mound. Add honey or date syrup into the small hole in the middle. Aseeda can be shaped into hearts, stars, moons and any other shapes. Before using cookie cutters, make sure to rub melted butter on top of the Aseeda to make cookie cutting easier. Aseeda can be eaten with fingers or a spoon. Dough is dipped into the honey and date syrup.

Kristin Machuta's Pan Fry

When I was a little girl my family lived with my grandmother in an old farm house in Yelm, Washington, USA. In total there were around twelve people living in the house, six of us being kids. While everyone always had a full belly and we were always warm, I can distinctly remember family commenting on money being tight. So many of our meals were things that could be stretched to feed the many bellies in the house or if we had left over they'd be things we could turn into something else. Like roast beef or chicken can be used to make soup or pies.

During the time we lived with my grandmother I have fond memories of her making up a dish that we all came to call a 'Pan Fry'. It consisted of potatoes, onions, garlic, butter, cheese, eggs and either chopped bacon, ham or breakfast sausage. As time went on and we all moved away the members of my family started putting their own twist on this with various mix-ins, but I will always prefer the classic.

Now the ratios for this dish aren't exact, as they're all to taste or to what you have in your cabinets, but here's a rough ratio on what you'll need to make a breakfast for two or three people. I hope you enjoy this cheap and filling dish!

Ingredients

4 Large washed potatoes
1 Onion, sliced into half moons or diced to preferred size
1 Garlic clove, minced
1 Cup cooked chopped Bacon, Ham or cooked Breakfast sausage.
4 Eggs
Butter, as much as you feel necessary. (Olive oil can be used but it's not as nice)
Shredded cheese of your choice

Microwave potatoes until are cooked all the way through. Let cool, then peel and cut into bite sized chunks.

In a large frying pan put in potatoes, onion, garlic and butter. Fry until potatoes at just under medium heat until they develop a golden brown crust and onions are cooked through. (Level of heat varies stove to stove. Use your judgement on this one.)

Over this dump in your cooked bacon/ham/sausage and then pour whisked egg over the top and sprinkle in some of your cheese.

Carefully turn the mixture over with a spatula until cooked all the way through, then top with your remaining cheese. Be careful not to squish your potatoes.

Tada! You have a hearty and filling Pan Fry.

I have cousins that like to put chunky salsa or ketchup on top of theirs.

It's highly customizable! Eat it as is. Use it in breakfast burritos. Bake it in a cast iron skillet for frittatas or use it as a quiche filling.

I do hope you all enjoy this recipe and put your own family twist to the dish!

Daniel Goli

My name is Daniel. I am 26 years old and I was born in Brisbane to an Australian mother and Iranian father. My older sister and I grew up in Brisbane but travelled to Iran on holidays growing up to visit family, which helped us to maintain an interest in and connection with our heritage and Iranian culture.

Both my father and mother cooked growing up however, my sister and I were always particularly fond of the Iranian dishes prepared by my father. No dish was more special than chelo kabob – a traditional and quintessential Iranian meal consisting of steamed long-grain rice and one of the many varieties of Iranian kabob, usually accompanied by grilled tomatoes, fresh herbs, yoghurt with cucumber and dried herbs, and pickled or fresh vegetables.

My father would cook this dish on special occasions or when guests were over, meaning it was always a treat when we had the opportunity to feast on our favourite meal.

A lot of effort goes into preparing and cooking chelo kabob; however, it is an experience that brings people together and the extra effort is well worth it. This recipe will be for my favourite kabob – joojeh (chicken). Making Chelo Kabob starts by preparing the meat the night before you plan to cook, allowing it to marinate overnight and absorb lots of flavour!

Chelo Kabob

Preparing the Joojeh

1 to 1.5 KG of thigh fillets cut into chunks.
3-4 medium white onion minced finely in a food processor.
½ teaspoon of saffron threads ground into a powder in a mortar and pestle.
1 cup olive oil.
3 ripe limes; juiced (try to use ripe yellow limes as the juice is less acidic).
Salt and pepper.
Method
Combine all the ingredients in a large non-reactive pot and mix well so that the chicken is well coated with the onion/lime juice.
Cover and refrigerate overnight.

Preparing the Charcoal Grill

Kabobs are cooked on long, stainless-steel skewers lined vertically over a manghal – a portable stainless-steel charcoal grill. Start the charcoal with a couple of BBQ fire starters whilst preparing the skewers. The charcoal needs to be glowing red hot or the skewers will not cook through.

Preparing the Skewers

The skewers are long flat stainless steel about 2.5 cms wide, that are about 20 cms wider than the manghal, as the skewers rest on the sides of the manghal and are turned during cooking. Any shorter and you risk getting burnt fingers!
Skewer the marinated chicken so that the length of the kabob is about 5 cms less that the width of the manghal and is centered on the length of the skewer, so that there is enough room at each end of the skewer to sit over the charcoal on the manghal.
As you make each skewer, place it on a wide flat dish or tray so that you can carry it outside to the manghal.
Also skewer 3-4 whole ripe Roma tomatoes and 3-4 small capsicums on two separate skewers to the chicken.

Cooking the kabobs
Ensure that the charcoal in the manghal is glowing hot, when it is, you're ready to cook!
Rest the skewers over the charcoal by lining them vertically across the manghal.
Rotate the skewers every few minutes until all sides are cooked and slightly charred. Do the same for the tomatoes and capsicums.
Using a wide, shallow dish and a piece of noon (flatbread, like Lebanese pita) in one hand, remove the skewers from the manghal one at a time (be careful, the skewers will be hot!), placing the skewer over the dish with one hand and keeping it in place with the noon in your other hand as you pull the skewer out. The meat should slide off the skewer into the dish. Repeat for tomatoes and capsicum.

Cucumber Yoghurt (Mast-o-Khiar)

Cucumber yoghurt is served with many Iranian dishes but goes particularly well with kabob.

Grate 1 large cucumber and add to a bowl.
Mix in 2-3 cups of Greek yoghurt.
Add 2 tablespoons of dried herbs (usually dried mint, but you can also use any combination of dried basil, coriander, dill or parsley).
Top with a 3/4 of a teaspoon of dried rose petals (optional)

Serving

Serve the kabob with steamed rice on a plate, along with tomatoes, capsicum and a dollop cucumber yoghurt.

Kabob and rice can be accompanied by torshi (Iranian pickled vegetables) or dill pickles and raw red onion.

Chelo kabob is best enjoyed by mixing and matching the ingredients as you take a bite (a bit of rice and meat at the same time, followed by a spoonful of yoghurt, or some tomato and meat with a bite of pickled vegetable – it's up to you!).

Garlic Soy Chicken Wings

by Megan Little

Why did the chicken cross the road?
A question that has been pondered by generations of families, including mine. Year after year we would debate the answer, always with speculation but never with certainty. Little did we know, the answer was right in front of us the whole time.
Garlic soy Chicken Wings! Surely this was the purpose of the chicken. Surely the chicken crossed the road so that our family could pass down from generation to generation a simple but succulent recipe for mouth watering garlic soy Chicken Wings. I can remember having many a tough time, sad night or hard day where I would turn to the love and fun I would have cooking this recipe with my family. Making the difficult times easier and the easy times amazing. Cooking with my family has always been so important to us. The safety and comfort that comes with the feeling of creating a dish together is something I will absolutely share with my children when the time comes. So I ask you; why did the chicken cross the road in your family?

Ingredients

1kg of wing nibbles
Garlic salt
Pepper
1 x bottle of soy sauce
1 x cup of lemonade

Method

Pat dry wings with paper towel and place in a medium sized bowl
Sprinkle garlic salt and pepper over the wings and toss to coat
Bring frying pan to medium high heat
Pour lemonade into frying pan until the base is covered and the wings would almost be covered
This may be more than 1 x cup
Pour soy sauce up and down the frying pan to cover
Place wings in frying pan
Cover wings in soy sauce
Cook for approx. 10 minutes with the lid on
Flip wings and cook for another approx. 10 minutes with lid on
Take lid off and cook while moving wings around in the pan
The liquid will start to caramelise. If burning, add a small amount of lemonade and turn down heat as required
Take wings off heat and allow to cool before consuming

Lorenzo Halim

I came to Australia in 2019 as one of the last international students before Corona Virus came to Australia in mid-February. I was raised with the influence of diverse religions in an inland mountain area of Chile.

Since moving here, if I can answer this question genuinely, the experience has been liberating, safe, but isolating at the same time. I have met amazing people from all over the world but at the expense of being unable to see my family for about two years. They have been hospitalised recently because of the insurgence of Corona Virus.

In Australia, I am able to express myself freely and celebrate my own personal values. It has been tough to survive without any support from the government and since I am still not a permanent resident, they have lots of restrictions Imposed on me.

But enough of that! The positive things in Australia has been the ability to enjoy the diverse melting pot of cultures and the pristine beaches. Also, to make very close connections during tough times and assist others who have had a similar experience to mine. Lastly, I have been able to taste lots of diverse foods since my journey to Australia.

My favourite dish would be Pecel. I make this by myself. The dish is very easy to make, rich in protein and low in calories. It signifies practicality, simplicity, and travel since the dish is often found along the train journey across Java.

Here is a list of the most commonly used vegetables in a Pecel; spinach, cabbage, Kangkung (morning glory/water spinach), bean sprouts, snake beans, cucumber, Daun Kemangi (basil leaves), and cassava leaves. Some people love to add crackers to their Pecel and the most common one is Rempeyek Kacang (peanut crackers), but this is purely optional.

Pecel

Peanut Sauce

250-gram peanuts with skin on (Indonesian: kacang tanah kulit), deep fried or toasted
8 red cayenne peppers (Indonesian: cabe merah keriting), boiled (*)
4 cloves garlic (Indonesian: bawang putih), fried
8 kaffir lime leaves (Indonesian: daun jeruk), thinly sliced
2-inch kaempferia galanga (Indonesian: kencur), peeled
1 teaspoon toasted shrimp paste (Indonesian: terasi)
75-gram palm sugar (Indonesian: gula Jawa), shaved
1/2 tablespoon salt
2 tablespoon tamarind juice (1 teaspoon tamarind + 2 tablespoon water)
enough hot water to thin the sauce (about 2 cups)

Suggested Vegetables

boiled cabbage (Indonesian: kol)
boiled spinach (Indonesian: bayam)
boiled snake beans (Indonesian: kacang panjang)
boiled bean sprouts (Indonesian: tauge)
boiled morning glory/water spinach (Indonesian: kangkung)
boiled cassava leaves (Indonesian: daun singkong)
raw cucumber (Indonesian: timun)
raw basil leaves (Indonesian: daun kemangi)

Instructions

Grind together peanuts, cayenne peppers, garlic, kaffir lime leaves, kaempferia galanga, toasted shrimp paste, palm sugar, and salt with a food processor (or mortar and pestle) until everything comes together into a thick brown mess. It will be pretty sticky and should clump together and you should be able to gather them into a ball or shape into a block. This can be stored in the fridge if you are not going to use the peanut sauce immediately.
To make the peanut sauce, pour tamarind juice and just enough hot water and stir until the sauce reaches your preferred thickness. I am usually happy with about 400 ml of hot water, but some people would prefer a slightly thicker or slightly thinner sauce, so feel free to experiment.
Arrange vegetables in a plate and pour the peanut sauce right before serving. Stir everything together and enjoy.

Note - If you like spicier peanut sauce, you can substitute some of the cayenne peppers with bird eye peppers (Indonesian: cabe rawit).

Julie Fischart

Culturally I am South African born to Welsh parents, 26 years spent in South Africa growing up in small coal and steel works town. My adult years I have spent in Australia (which we call home) but in that time I have also lived many years in the Middle East. I love the diversity of all the cultures and have learnt so many great recipes but today I will be making a South African, Cape Malay dish called Bobotie. It is believed that the dish is from Malayan or Indonesian origin possibly appearing first in a Dutch recipe book in 1609.

In 1996, with a husband, two toddlers aged two and five and with 13 bags of luggage we said goodbye to family and friends in Johannesburg, South Africa and boarded a plane to Brisbane, Australia!"

It was a country we had never been to but with limited internet in those days we researched as much as we could and liked what we saw. So, we lined up some interviews for my husband and took a chance.

Saying goodbye to family and friends in South Africa was horrendous and I remember saying to my husband after we had arrived, I really hope this decision was worth the pain.

Well 25 years later and with Aussie born son number 3 and a lifetime of wonderful memories I can safely say we took a gamble and it worked for us.

The freedom of parks and the absolutely stunning beaches made many a family outing so much fun.

Taken at Bourkes Luck Potholes Blyde River Canyon Nature Reserve Moremela, South Africa 1991

Bobotie

Prep time 15 mins
Cook time 35
Serves 2-4

Ingredients

1tbsp olive oil
350g lean mince
1 onion, finely chopped
1 garlic clove, crushed
2 tbsp curry powder
2 tbsp korma paste
1 large carrot, grated
1 granny smith apple, grated
2 tbsp Mrs Ball's Chutney (can be found in any good SA items shop)
1 tbsp cider vinegar
Handful of raisins
2 eggs
375ml milk
1 slice white bread
1 bay leaf

Method

Heat oven 160c fan forced cook 25-30 min
Break up bread into pieces and pour over 125ml of milk, leave to soak
Heat oil in a large pan and add mince to brown, breaking up with a wooden spoon. 4.
Add chopped onion, garlic, curry powder and korma paste.
Add grated carrot and apple, Mrs Balls chutney, cider vinegar and raisins. Add a little hot water and simmer for 8-10 minutes (adding more water if needed) until raisins have swelled and carrot softened.
Season with salt and black pepper.
Mix remaining milk and and eggs together until well combined
Add bread to mince and mash in well until it is no longer visible.
Spoon the mince mixture into an oven proof dish spreading evenly.
Pour egg and milk (egg custard) over the mince placing the bay leaf in the middle
Back in the oven for 25-30 minutes or until the egg custard has set.
Serve with samba and a salad
Side note: I have made a vegetarian version using lentils instead of mince and soya milk, with gluten free bread and a gluten free chutney following the same basic steps of the recipe.

Atiya Karimshah

Cooking was the way women bonded in my culture. Not just in the home but in the community. Some of my most vivid memories from my childhood are associated with cooking. Sundays spent in the kitchen with my mother, and sister, music blaring as we danced and sang and laughed. The women gathering in the week leading up to a wedding to peel vegetables while they told dirty jokes about carrots.
Cooking the roti at my Nanna's house for Friday family lunch while my aunties rolled them out and checked on the pots that had been cooking since morning.

My paternal grandmother was like a mad scientist in the kitchen as she cooked half remembered recipes from her childhood that often included ingredients like cows tongue and sheep's brain.

My mother meticulously typed out recipes on her typewriter in triplicate so my sister and I would each have a recipe book when we grew up.

I had two maternal grandmothers. Both of them cooked by touch, no recipe needed. This is how I cook.

My mothers and her sisters all had handwritten recipe books that they shared with each other. They always wrote down the name of the person they copied the recipe from. So their recipe books had recipes like "Shazia's chocolate cake" and "Api Nasreens Beat and Bake."

My mother sent me a photo of this recipe for Kebabs, it was handwritten by her sister, who copied it out of their mothers old recipe book before it fell apart. The recipe probably didn't need to be written down because its in our genetic memory at this point but the sentiment of preserving it was there.

This recipe is a family favorite and is always found on the table at special occasions. I cook it when I'm feeling nostalgic about the extra long kitchen table in my grandfather's house half a world away, where my aunties are probably rolling out roti's and checking on the pots that have cooking since morning.

Khan Family Kebabs

1 Kg Beef Mince
1 Tbsp Red Chilli
1 Tbsp Minced Garlic,
1 Tbsp crushed Ginger
1 Tbsp Cumin and Corriander powder
3-4 Spring onions chopped
A few chillies chopped
1 Medium sized brown onion grated
1 bunch of fresh Coriander finely chopped
2 slices of white bread

Soak the bread in water until completely saturated then squeeze out any excess water. Thoroughly mix all the ingredient togetherin a large bowl.

This recipe is ideal when cooked on a skewer over the barbaque but is also just as declicious when cooked in a frying with a little oil.

Serve with chutney or sauce of your choice.

Tiwi Suprihani

Indonesian people love eating food. We have so many varieties of food, we always have rice for breakfast, lunch and dinner, we call rice; nasi. We have Nasi Goreng, (Fried Rice) Nasi Ayam, Nasi Rames (nasi with so many dishes), Nasi Gudeg, Nasi Padang , Nasi Kuning etc. We always enjoy food. In the morning so many people sell snacks, so many varieties of snacks you can choose from because we always have snacks after breakfast.

I love cooking, I had a snack business. Everyday I made snacks, Sosis Solo (like a spring roll, but pastry made from egg and flour, filled with chicken), Risoles, Kue Lapis (rainbow cake from rice flour) etc.

Every morning my mother always made breakfast. Sometimes she made Nasi Goreng. It is my favorite breakfast. I loved it when my mother made Nasi Goreng, just simple Nasi Goreng. She just put a little bit of green chillies, garlic, onion, green onion, egg, and salt.

Sometimes I put in chicken or prawns. Here in Australia, I miss the Nasi Goreng my mother made and I try to cook Nasi Goreng like her, but the taste is not the same as my mother's.

I love noodles too. In Indonesia every night many people sell food. Nasi Goreng, Ayam Goreng (fried chicken with sambal), Ayam Bakar (grill chicken with charcoal fire and sambal) and Mie Goreng (fried noodle), Mie Godong (boiled noodle with soup) and the taste is amazing.

It is delicious and smells very nice because they cook bakkmi (noodles) on a charcoal fire. I always miss this food. You can find Ikan Bakar (Grilled Fish on a charcoal fire), Satai, Gado Gado, Pecel (mix vegetables with peanuts sauce) and so many other foods you can get on the street, very cheap and delicious.

Nasi Goreng

1 plate of white rice
2 cloves garlic, finely chopped
Sweet soy sauce or soy sauce according to taste
Chili sauce according to taste
oyster sauce to taste
Salt
To taste chicken or beef flavor powder
1 green onion finely chopped
1 egg
1 chicken sausage, thinly sliced
100 gr prawn
2 crab sticks.. cut to be 4
Margarine or cooking oil 3 tbsp

How to make :

Prepare a frying pan over medium heat, pour margarine or cooking oil.
Add the finely chopped onion and garlic. Saute until fragrant or until golden in color.
Add sausage and 1 chicken egg. Prawn Saute briefly.
Add ground spices and rice. Stir until well blended.
Pour in the sweet soy sauce, chili sauce, oyster sauce, salt, and powdered stock. Stir until the color of the rice changes evenly.
Add crab sticks, fried rice is ready to be served.

Katrina Patindol

My family comes from Philippines and I was born in Sydney, Australia. Growing up in Sydney I would see my friends living with their mum, dad and siblings where my household was always full, from siblings, to grandparents to aunties, uncles and cousins. I grew up in a very collective family and culture, where you would know the people down the street in the Philippines but growing up in Australia, people barely talk to their next-door neighbor. The food was also very different, rice was never at fast food restaurants in Australia where in Philippines its an option to swap for fries!

Growing up, my favorite dish to eat was Kare-Kare (Oxtail & Tripe stew in Peanut Sauce)

Many people in my family have **tried** to cook this dish, but no one would cook it like my Grandfather would. He would make enough to feed his wife, 11 kids, 18 grandkids and extra for people on the streets

This dish was so special because my grandfather would only make it on special occasions, which to him was birthdays and whenever I would request the dish, but also because he would always make it the way I like it even if the rest of the family didn't enjoy it as much.

Kare Kare's cultural significance was first introduced during the Spanish era and would only be served to royalty and elite as oxtail was very hard to come by back then. Then again, my grandfather also told me that the Spanish took the term Kare Kare from the Indian word curry many years before that.

Kare Kare

2 pounds oxtail – cut into cubes
1 pound oxtail tripe (edible lining from oxtail stomach) - cut into pieces
6 cups of water
2 tablespoons of oil
2 cloves garlic – minced
1 medium onion – chopped
6 pieces yard-long beans-ends trimmed and cut into 3-inch pieces
1 small banana heart – cut and presoaked
2 medium eggplants – cut into 2-inch pieces
2 tablespoons annatto powder
1 cup peanut butter
Half teaspoon of salt
Quarter cup sticky rice flour
Half a cup of shrimp paste
3 medium bok choy

Simmer Cook Oxtail, Tripe, water, garlic and onions for 2.5 - 3 hours or until meat is tender.

Saute bok choy, eggplant and banana heart in a seperate pan

Add all other ingredients to the oxtail mixture and simmer for a few minutes

Add sauted vegetables.

Serve.

Sangeeta Mehta

Food and recipes make a great link to connect the past and future generations.

Over 30 years ago, my husband and I migrated to Australia from India to start a life together in Australia. We yearned for the foods we grew up with.

We would reminisce about the flavours and the stories attached to many of the favourite dishes which defined childhood for us. One such dish was Butter Chicken.

My mother doesn't appreciate non-vegetarian food being brought into the main kitchen. My father relished making this dish in his little kitchenette out in the courtyard. Scurrying to the main kitchen to fetch 'that one missing spice' would make us kids feel very important!

Home away from home, reliving childhood memories; my husband perfected his spin on a family favourite.

I loved making this quick version as it didn't compromise on taste.

It became our go-to after a day's work, when we needed something simple, yet satisfying. Being a crowd pleaser, it earned a place of pride on our dinner menus when friends came over.

It became a family favourite for more reasons than one!

Far away from families, food paved the way for us to teach our children about their Indian heritage and values of our land.

Butter Chicken always brought the dining table alive with conversations. Their stories made us aware about different ways of raising children in other cultures. We taught them about our heritage, trying to strike a balance between the values of our homeland and our chosen land. What would start as a simple meal, invariably ended up being lessons in life, learning tolerance and respect for all cultures and cuisines.

It's memories like these which gives this recipe a special place on our dining table.

Even now, when our young adults come home for the joys of comfort food, we revel in being able to share another slice of our culture with them – one bite at a time.

I am sure Butter Chicken will feature on their dining tables too.

One day; they may even use it to pass our culture on to the next generation.

Preparation time-15min
Cooking time-30 min

4 Chicken thigh fillets, halved
1 cup tomato puree
1 cup tomato ketchup
¼ cup thick cream
50gm salted butter
1 pinch saffron(soaked in tepid water) or orange food colour
Salt and White pepper to taste
1 tsp dry fenugreek leaves(if available)
2 tblsp chopped fresh coriander

Seal chicken in a hot (thick, heavy base) pan with a little butter. Keep aside.
Add the remaining butter, tomato puree and ketchup to the pan. Bring to a boil. Reduce to half.
Add all other ingredients except cream and coriander.
Cover and cook till the chicken is tender.
Add cream. Bring to a boil.
Garnish with coriander.
Serve hot with steamed rice/Indian bread.

Vegetarian Variation: Instead of chicken, use 1 cup of cubed, grilled Paneer (Indian cottage cheese) and 1/2 cup of frozen peas.

Maria Iskander

Growing up in a traditional Coptic Orthodox household, home cooking- among attending Liturgical services, was very much a part of the daily routine. To add, at the time, acquiring Egyptian cooking cuisines was an exclusive expectation for both males and females in my family; gender equality - and it still is.

These recipes are close to my heart because I learned them from my great uncle and Coptic Orthodox priest- Fr Moussa Soliman. The first being the Kahk biscuit recipe, which is made twice a year at local churches, for Easter and Christmas celebrations. The second, being the omelette recipe, is made for luxury breakfasts on the weekends.

Currently , Fr Moussa Soliman serves the Coptic Orthodox community in Sydney. Hence, with the millions of people, nationwide, forced to stay at home and limit travel; these recipes have found a new meaning for me. Not only do they celebrate my rich Egyptian culture, but they help alleviate the pain of distance I have with my family interstate and overseas.

Nevertheless, when you are cooking these recipes, I hope that you think of it as an enjoyable and a tasty "choose your own adventure" experience.

Kahk Biscuits

For the agameya (honey filling) - results in 20 – 24 pieces
1 Tablespoon ghee (clarified butter)
1/8 cup all-purpose flour
6 Tablespoons honey
½ Tablespoon sesame seeds, toasted
2 Tablespoon finely chopped almonds (or other nut of choice)

For the date (Agwa) filling – results in 20 – 24 pieces
120 g (roughly 1/2 cup) pitted Medjool dates (other dates can also be used)
1 Tablespoon butter (or ghee)
1/2 teaspoon cinnamon powder

For the Kahk dough – results in about 44 – 48 cookies
½ kg (4 cups) all- purpose flour
1 teaspoon baking powder
1/8 teaspoon salt
1/2 teaspoon cinnamon powder*
300 g (1 1/3 cups) ghee (clarified butter)
50 g (1/2 cup) powdered sugar / icing sugar, for dusting
½ cup milk

Use a tablespoon to scoop out the dough and roll between your palms to form individual balls. The dough balls should be double the size of the filling balls. (It is important to make sure the dough balls are all the same size, so that they bake evenly.)

To make the agameya (honey filling)

Melt the ghee in a small saucepan over medium-high heat. Add the flour and cook till the mixture turns light golden brown. Make sure to whisk constantly with a small whisk.

Add honey and bring to a boil. Make sure to stir constantly. Once the mixture comes to a boil, turn heat to low-medium, and cook till the honey starts to thicken. The consistency should be of a thick pourable sauce, but not hardened. If a candy thermometer is available, this is what is called the soft ball stage, 234-240F (112-116C). Remove the saucepan from the heat and add the toasted sesame seeds along with the finely chopped nuts. Stir through, and then transfer the agameya to a small bowl. Let the mixture cool till it is firm, but still soft enough to shape. In the case the mixture hardens too much, warm it in the microwave for a few seconds.

Grease hands with oil, and then roll the agameya into small teaspoon sized balls. Use a small cookie scoop or teaspoon to help with scooping out the filling. Place the agameya balls on a parchment paper lined tray and keep in the fridge until ready to use.

For the date (agwa) filling

Place the pitted Medjool dates in a food processor, and pulse until a paste is formed. If a food processor isn't available, it is possible to chop the dates finely using a sharp knife.

Place butter in a small saucepan over low heat and let it melt.

Add the chopped dates along with the cinnamon powder and stir together.

Stir the dates till a soft paste is formed. If necessary, add ½ - 1 tablespoon of water.

Once the paste is formed, take the dates out of the saucepan, and let the paste cool.

Once the date paste is cool, make small teaspoon sized balls of the date mixture. Just like you did with the agameya filling. (Grease your hands with oil if necessary.) Place the date paste balls on a parchment paper lined tray and keep in the fridge until ready to use.

For the Kahk dough

Place the flour, cinnamon powder, baking powder and salt in a bowl. Mix with a spoon and set aside.

Place ghee (clarified butter) in a large bowl, and add the powdered sugar / icing sugar. Use an electric beater to whisk together till light and fluffy (about 2 minutes).

Add the flour mixture to the ghee and sugar. Mix with a wooden spoon until well combined. (The flour will get coated in the ghee / clarified butter and have a crumbly texture.)

Add the milk and mix again. The dough is ready when it can be formed into a ball and doesn't crack when pressed. In case the dough hasn't come together, add another tablespoon of milk or a tablespoon of flour, as required.

Cover the dough with a cloth, and let it rest it in a cool place or the refrigerator for about 30 minutes.

Just before you start to roll your cookies, preheat your oven to 180 C (355F) and line two baking sheets with parchment paper.

Use a tablespoon to scoop out the dough and roll between your palms to form individual balls. The dough balls should be double the size of the filling balls. (It is important to make sure the dough balls are all the same size, so that they bake evenly.)

Egyptian Feta Cheese Omelette Roll

4 eggs, beaten
½ teaspoon black pepper
3 tablespoons crumbled feta cheese
1 teaspoon milk
1 tablespoon vegetable oil

In a small bowl, beat eggs and pepper together. In another small bowl, combine crumbled cheese with milk.

Heat oil in a large non-stick skillet over medium-high heat. Pour in eggs, and tilt pan until bottom is evenly covered. When edges appear cooked, place feta mixture in a line in the centre of eggs. Using a spatula, fold eggs over top and bottom of cheese, then fold sides over.

Lamb Curry Bunny Chow

By Samanthra Govender

Hailing from South Africa but showcasing a strong Indian heritage, curry featured dominantly as a staple dish in our household. Growing up these dishes were often treats and I recall weekends happily spent with family together enjoying these delicious curries cooked by my Amma (mother).

Here's the recipe for Lamb Curry Bunny Chow

Ingredients I use: (I'm not a hard stickler for ingredients and quantities so feel free to adjust accordingly)

500g lamb cut into pieces
4 tbsp oil
1 large onion chopped
¼ tsp turmeric
1 sprig curry leaf
½ tbsp chilli seeds
2 tsp ginger crushed finely
2 tsp garlic paste
4 tbsp masala
1 medium tomato chopped
4-6 potatoes cut in half
3 sprigs fresh coriander (dhunya)
salt to taste
water

This is how I go about cooking the curry. You can use the exact same process for chicken curry or mince curry!
Heat oil and then add onion, turmeric & curry leaves and fry for a few seconds (allow onion to soften)
Add masala, ginger & garlic, chilli seeds and allow to cook for a few seconds (do not burn masala)
Add tomato
Stir in meat and fry up. Allow to cook for 15-20minutes.
Add potatoes and water as it cooks.
Turn down to moderate heat and cover saucepan.
Cook until meat is tender & potatoes are soft.
Simmer until ready to serve and garnish with chopped dhunya.
Serve curry with roti, steamed rice or fresh bread.

Also by 1000 Tales

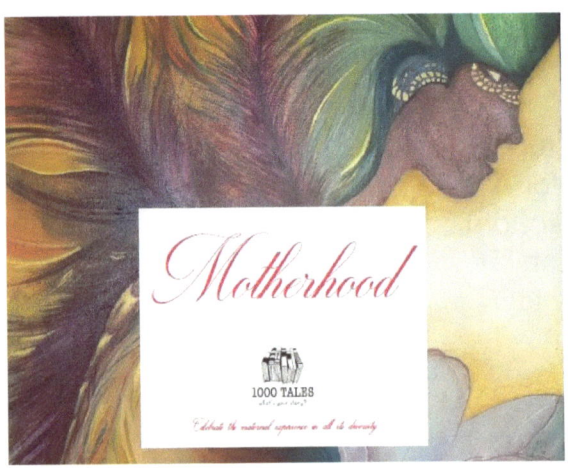